Tricky Tarantulas

Alex Kuskowski
AUTHOR

C.A. Nobens
ILLUSTRATOR

Consulting Editor, Diane Craig, M.A./Reading Specialist

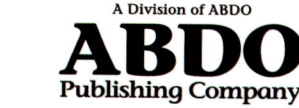

visit us at www.abdopublishing.com

Published by ABDO Publishing Company, a division of ABDO, P.O. Box 398166, Minneapolis, Minnesota 55439. Copyright © 2013 by Abdo Consulting Group, Inc. International copyrights reserved in all countries. No part of this book may be reproduced in any form without written permission from the publisher. SandCastle™ is a trademark and logo of ABDO Publishing Company.

Printed in the United States of America, North Mankato, Minnesota
102012
012013

 PRINTED ON RECYCLED PAPER

Editor: Liz Salzmann
Content Developer: Nancy Tuminelly
Cover and Interior Design and Production: Kelly Doudna, Mighty Media, Inc.
Photo Credits: iStockPhoto (Jake Holmes, Daniel Laflor), Shutterstock

Library of Congress Cataloging-in-Publication Data

Kuskowski, Alex.
  Tricky tarantulas / by Alex Kuskowski ; illustrator C.A. Nobens.
     p. cm. -- (Unusual pets)
  ISBN 978-1-61783-402-8
  1. Tarantulas as pets--Juvenile literature. I. Nobens, C. A., ill. II. Title.
SF459.T37K87 2013
595.4'4--dc23
                                    2011050813

SandCastle™ Level: Transitional

SandCastle™ books are created by a team of professional educators, reading specialists, and content developers around five essential components—phonemic awareness, phonics, vocabulary, text comprehension, and fluency—to assist young readers as they develop reading skills and strategies and increase their general knowledge. All books are written, reviewed, and leveled for guided reading, early reading intervention, and Accelerated Reader® programs for use in shared, guided, and independent reading and writing activities to support a balanced approach to literacy instruction. The SandCastle™ series has four levels that correspond to early literacy development. The levels are provided to help teachers and parents select appropriate books for young readers.

Emerging Readers
(no flags)

Beginning Readers
(1 flag)

Transitional Readers
(2 flags)

Fluent Readers
(3 flags)

Contents

Unusual Pets 4
Tarantula Basics 5
Tarantulas 6
A Tarantula Story 14
Fun Facts 22
Tarantula Quiz 23
Glossary 24

Unusual Pets

Unusual pets can be interesting and fun! Unusual pets might also eat unusual food. They might have special care needs. It is a good idea to learn about your new friend before bringing it home.

There are special laws for many unusual animals. Make sure the kind of pet you want is allowed in your city and state.

Tarantula Basics

Type of animal
Tarantulas are **arachnids**.

Adult size
1 to 3 ounces (28 to 85 g)

Life expectancy
6 to 14 years

Natural habitat
in **burrows** and tree trunks, and on the ground

Ethan's pet tarantula likes to stay in her **tank**. If Ethan wants to take her out, he has to be very careful.

Tarantulas want places to hide. Sadie's tarantula crawls into a log.

Tarantulas eat small insects. Crickets are their favorite.

Rob looks closely at his tarantula. The hairs of a tarantula sense odors, touches, and temperature.

A Tarantula Story

Jackson Lee has a pet.
He is unlike any other.
He keeps him in his room,
so he doesn't scare his mother!

Jackson's pet is a tarantula.
That's a kind of spider.
His mom screams real loud
when he sits beside her!

He's big and black and **fuzzy**.
He stays awake at night.
He climbs out of his **tank**
when Jackson's sleeping tight.

Houdini is the perfect name.
He always gets away.
Most often in the dark,
but sometimes in the day.

When the spider disappears,
Jackson's fairly certain
he can look up and find
Houdini on the **curtain**!

One day Jackson looks around.
But he just can't find Houdini.
Then he hears a scream
from his little sister Jeannie!

He hurries to her side.
He sees the spider on the floor.
Houdini has been sitting
beside her dollhouse door.

Jackson picks Houdini up.
He puts him in his home.
Jackson makes Houdini safe,
so now he cannot roam.

Fun Facts

* Tarantula bites hurt, but are not deadly to people.

* Young tarantulas **shed** their skin in order to grow.

* There are more than 800 different kinds of tarantulas.

* Tarantulas get their name from the town of Taranto in Italy.

* Some wild tarantulas spin webs that look like **hammocks**.

Tarantula Quiz

Read each sentence below. Then decide whether it is true or false!

1. Ethan has to be careful with his tarantula.

2. Sadie's tarantula is under a rock.

3. Tarantulas eat insects.

4. Jackson's mom says hello when Houdini sits beside her.

5. Jackson finds Houdini next to a dollhouse.

Answers: 1. True 2. False 3. True 4. False 5. True

Glossary

arachnid – a small creature with eight legs, no antennae, and a body with two sections. Spiders, scorpions, and ticks are arachnids.

burrow – a hole or tunnel dug in the ground by a small animal for shelter.

curtain – a large piece of cloth that can be pulled across a window or a stage.

fuzzy – covered with hair or fur.

hammock – a net or cloth hung by cords at each end so that you can lie on it.

shed – to lose something, such as skin, leaves, or fur, through a natural process.

tank – a large container for fish or small animals to live in.

J595.44 Kus
Kuskowski, Alex.
Tricky tarantulas